Collect it!

Making collections – from fossils to fakes

Elizabeth Newbery
Illustrations by Robert Geary

Contents

So you're a collector	2
Why not branch out?	4
It's a collector's world	8
Going out to collect	16
Getting sorted	22
Caring for your collection	24
Modern museums	36
Fabulous fakes	39
How to find out more	44

A & C Black · London

So you're a collector

Most people collect something during their lives. Do you? You may collect something easily available like car stickers or shells, or something that doesn't last very long, like leaves. As you grow older you might like to collect something a bit unusual or something which might gain in value.

Did you know that some of our most famous museums, libraries and art galleries were once someone's collection? You could start your own museum. Why not?

Before this book was written, young people were asked if they collected anything and what it was.

Coins

Have you ever picked up a coin and wondered what it would tell you if it could speak? This old penny may have jingled around in the pocket of someone the same age as you nearly a hundred years ago.

People collect coins for many reasons: coins of a particular country perhaps, or coins which bear pictures of animals or ships. Some people collect coins for their value; if you have chosen your coins carefully it may be possible to sell them for more than they originally cost.

The best way to start collecting coins is to ask your family and friends if they have any old coins they no longer want. Perhaps they spent holidays abroad and have a few coins they can't exchange at a bank. Many junk shops have pots of worn coins all jumbled together. They are cheap to buy and might start off your collection.

Fossils, rocks and pebbles

Fossils, rocks and pebbles are the oldest things you can collect; most of them are millions of years old. Fossils are the shapes of plants and animals left in the rock. Millions of years ago, when the rock was soft mud or sand, leaves, shells and the bodies of dead animals fell into it and were slowly buried. Gradually the mud turned to rock and the shapes of the leaves, shells and animal bones hardened.

Different kinds of fossils come from different parts of the country, so go to your local library or museum to find out the best places to collect safely.

Stamps

Collecting stamps has always been popular. One of the most famous stamp collections in the world belongs to Queen Elizabeth II. It was started by her grandfather, King George V. The collection contains almost all the British Commonwealth stamps ever issued, from the 1p stamp which can be bought from your local Post Office to 1d and 2d (old money) stamps from Mauritius which are now worth thousands of pounds.

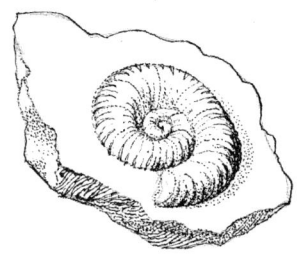

Does anyone else in your family collect anything? Maybe your parents have collected souvenirs of their holidays. Perhaps your grandparents collected something that you would not be allowed to collect today such as birds' eggs, wild flowers or archaeological remains.

What will happen to your collection? Will it be around for your grandchildren to look at? Here is what some young people said: 'I will give my football programmes to my grandsons and hope they will carry on.' 'I used to collect shells but my mum chucked them away.' 'My sister is thinking of turning my bedroom into a museum.'

Why not branch out?

Every day we throw away lots of unwanted paper items such as leaflets, packaging, old magazines and newspapers. How about collecting some of it? Most of this material is free, yet it is possible to build up an extremely interesting and sometimes valuable collection.

Dr John Johnson, who was in charge of the printing press at Oxford University over fifty years ago, saved all types of printed items including magazines, posters, programmes, games, coupons, leaflets, postcards, timetables and cartoons. The collection is now very important. It gives us details about the lives of ordinary people which would otherwise be lost for ever. After Dr Johnson died, his collection went to the Bodleian Library in Oxford. People from all over the world come to study it.

Most of us would not have the space to keep such a huge collection. So why not concentrate on one group of items? Robert Opie (below) concentrates on packaging and advertising materials, including labels, posters, and tins, boxes and mugs with advertisements on them. He now has over 250,000 items, a selection of which are in his own museum in Gloucester.

Every wrapper tells a story

Why not collect orange wrappers? Oranges, satsumas and clementines bought from markets are sometimes wrapped in flimsy tissue paper wrappers. Many have lively, colourful designs on them. Sometimes they tell us about things that are happening in the country where the oranges are packed. Orange wrappers can be collected free from markets at the end of the day, or at the most, for the price of an orange.

Ten million matchbox labels

What about matchbox labels? More than 10,000,000 labels have been produced, so it isn't difficult to pick up examples which no one else has.

Orange wrappers, matchbox labels, football programmes, stickers, magazines and all kinds of printed items – like those in Dr Johnson's collections – are called 'printed ephemera'. 'Ephemera' is a Greek word which means things that last only a short time. There is a society for people who collect printed ephemera. You can find the address on page 47.

A collection with its own ghost!

Do you own a dog? Does it wear a collar? Next time you buy a new collar and throw away the old one, think again! The 7th Lord Fairfax who lived over 200 years ago had three Great Dane dogs who looked especially handsome in large decorated collars. Lord Fairfax became interested in dog collars and started to collect them.

Today you can see his collection at Leeds Castle in Kent. It includes several large spiked collars which were worn by German hunting dogs to protect them from wild boar and stags. The collection even has its own ghost. A fiercesome hound called the Black Dog of Leeds Castle is said to appear to foretell bad luck!

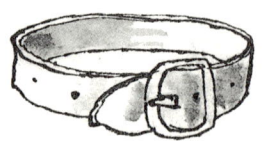

Button box treasures

Have you thought about collecting buttons? In the early 1720s a Frenchman called Philipe d'Orleans had a set of buttons made for himself which each contained a tiny watch. After that, wealthy Frenchmen competed with each other for the most luxurious buttons.

The first buttons were covered with embroidered fabric. Later they were made of many kinds of materials, from gold set with precious jewels to glass, wood and horn. Today, buttons are mostly made of plastic. You can pick up buttons very cheaply at street markets or jumble sales. Perhaps someone in your family has a button box containing a collection of buttons.

Ten green bottles

There were no bottle banks a hundred years ago. Although bottles were used over and over again, they couldn't be made into new objects as they can be today. The Victorians stored all sorts of things in bottles, from ginger beer to hair restorer – so there are thousands of bottles waiting to be collected all over the country. Some of them come in beautiful shapes and colours. Don't forget modern bottles. Next time you are in the supermarket look for things stored in bottles. Are any of them worth collecting?

Now you see it, now you don't

Because of new technology, many familiar things around us are becoming outdated and are fast disappearing. Old red telephone boxes are a good example. It would be difficult for you to collect telephone boxes, although some people do, but you could photograph them.

Coal hole covers were once a very common sight in pavements. They covered the entrance to delivery shutes for coal. What about 'collecting' them by making rubbings of them before they disappear altogether? Find out how to do this on page **20**.

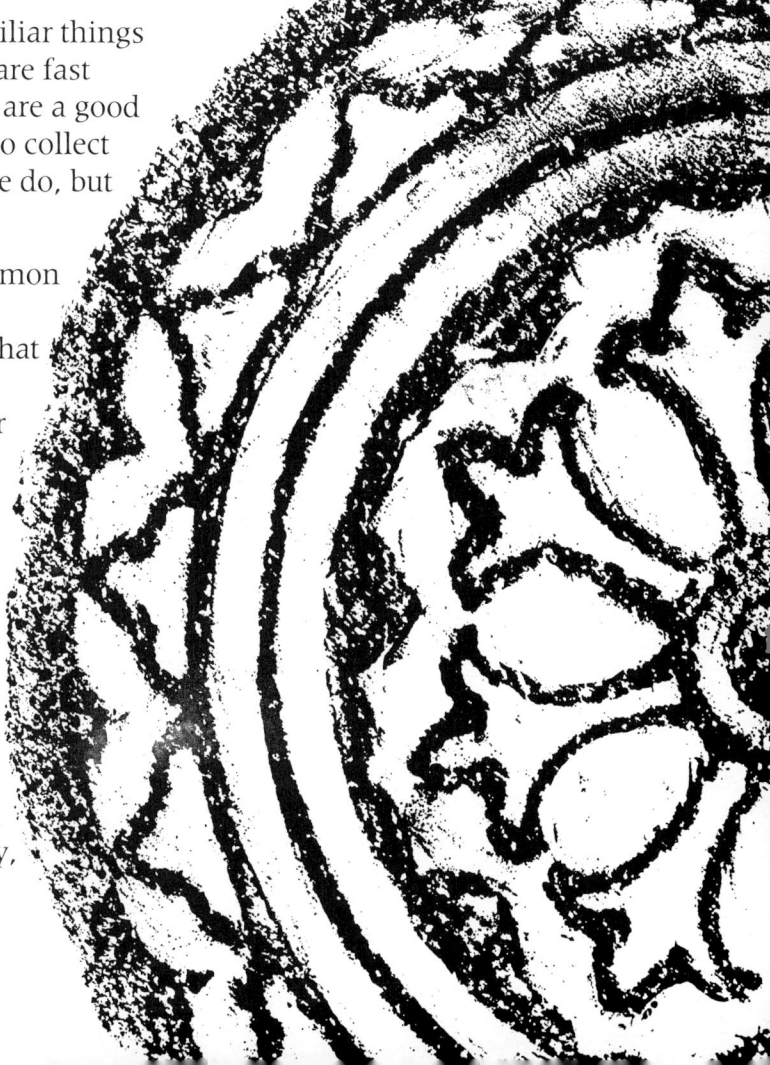

Collecting memories

Have you thought about collecting memories? What was it like for your grandparents during World War II? Perhaps you know of someone who remembers what it was like to live in a house without a bathroom or electricity, or someone who once lived in another country? Could you 'collect' their memories on tape?

It's a collector's world

There are collections of almost anything you can think of, from children's toys to chimney-pots. There is a pencil museum, a bagpipe museum and even a museum of crime! Are there any unusual collections in your area?

The Farmland Museum

Craig Delanoy was only four years old when he started to collect pieces of broken pottery which he picked up in his garden in Haddenham, Cambridgeshire. It was to be the start of his own museum. Craig called it the Farmland Museum because it was the best name he could make with his toy printing set which had many of the letters missing. From a shoe box, the collection expanded to fill a one-acre garden.

Twenty years later it is one of the most popular museums in the area, especially with young people. Craig, with the help of his father, collected a huge number of farming tools, veterinary and farming equipment, a blacksmith's forge, a harness-maker's shop and a collection of tools for crafts like basket-making and thatching.

The Brooking Collection

Charles Brooking was no more than three years old when he began to notice bits and pieces on houses. Today he has at least 25,000 items from buildings which he collects mainly from building sites. They include doors, windows, door knockers, letter plates, door handles, window fittings, staircases, rainwater heads, firegrates and wall-mounted post-boxes.

After many years in his parents' garden, his collection is now housed in The Thames Polytechnic. It is especially useful to people who are interested in restoring old houses. The picture above shows some of the objects in Charles Brooking's collection.

Snowshill Manor

Charles Wade was born in 1883. He lived with his grandmother who had a wonderful Chinese cabinet. The cabinet was only opened on Sunday afternoons and it was filled with family treasures. Charles was fascinated. He began to collect little oddments of his own with his pocket money. He became especially interested in objects skilfully made by hand.

When he was much older, Charles inherited a lot of money and eventually bought Snowshill Manor in Gloucestershire. He set about using the whole house to display his collection. He gave each of the rooms a name and a theme.

The room in the picture above is called 'Admiral' and contains objects to do with the sea. Other rooms were named after colours. The 'Turquoise Room' contained Charles's grandmother's cabinet which you can see on page **34**. What do you think the room called 'Dragon' contained?

Ulster Folk and Transport Museum

Some museums collect whole buildings! At the Ulster Folk and Transport Museum near Belfast in Northern Ireland you can see houses, public buildings, schools, workshops, farm buildings and two churches. They have all been rescued from destruction, carefully taken apart and re-erected in the museum. The museum also collects every kind of transport used in Ireland, and all the things people made and used in their everyday lives. It shows how people lived in Ireland about 100 years ago.

How does the museum go about collecting a building? First of all no building is brought into the museum if it can be saved where it is. Once the decision is taken to move a building, a group of specialist workers begin by making a very detailed survey and measuring everything. All the stones are numbered and then the building is photographed from all angles, inside and out. Samples are taken of the timber, usually the roof beams, so the date of the house can be worked out. Samples are also taken of the plaster, mortar and thatch so they can be matched up. Then the building is dismantled from the roof downwards, loaded on to lorries and moved to the museum.

On a carefully prepared site the builders can then begin to re-build the house, using the photographs as a guide, rather like the picture on the lid of a jig-saw puzzle.

Once the building is complete it is furnished with all the things that would have been in it 100 years ago. It can then be used to show people how their ancestors lived. In Ballyveridagh School in these pictures, schoolchildren can now find out what it was like to be in a Victorian classroom.

1. Baleyveridagh National School as it stood near Ballycastle before the Museum began work on it.

2. All the stones were carefully numbered, the buildings were then photographed, dismantled and the stones moved to the Museum.

Museum in Docklands

Chris Ellmers (left) collects for the Museum in Docklands which is part of the Museum of London. About ten years ago Chris realised that many of the things to do with the River Thames, the docks and the river trades and industries which had grown up alongside it, were disappearing fast as the area changed. Chris and a small team of helpers have collected enough objects to fill several warehouses. It is the largest collection of material from a working port and river in the world. It includes boats, different types of containers, custom sheds, beam engines, cranes and thousands of signs. There are anchors, buoys, blocks and pulleys and even a special barrow for carting off injured dockers to hospital!

Rebuilding work in progress.

A view of the completed front of the school.

But the collection isn't all objects. Chris also looks after 20,000 photographs of the port at work, 30,000–40,000 architectural and engineering plans and drawings, 10,000 books and 600 hours of tape, recording the memories of over 200 older men and women who once worked in the London docks.

A family museum

In the past many families made their own museums. The Yorke children who lived in a house called Erdigg, near Wrexham in Wales, were helped by the family butler, Dickinson, to catch, chloroform and mount butterflies (something which wouldn't be allowed today). The children displayed them in the family museum in the basement of the house. The museum also contained a collection of old coins, fragments of Chinese figurines, a swordfish blade, Indian bus tickets, a hornet's nest and a highly polished skull!

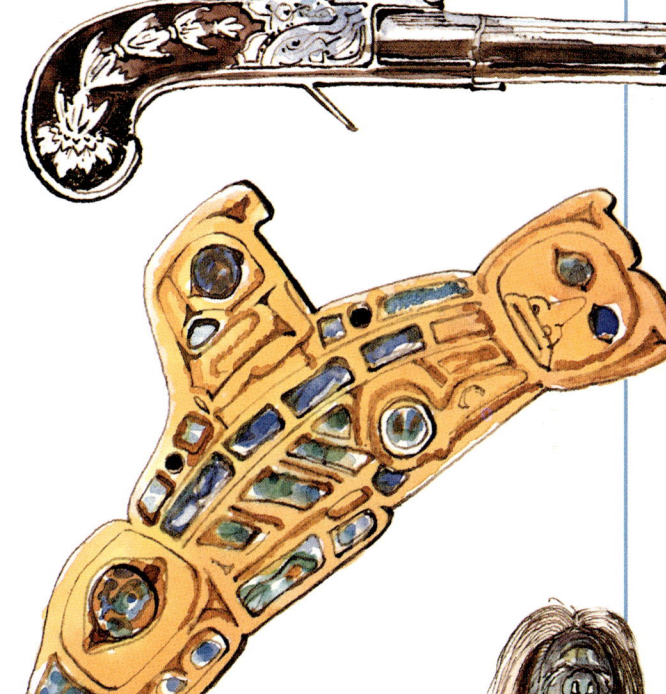

A collector of clues

Lieutenant General Pitt Rivers (above) collected clues. He was one of the first people to realise that objects could tell us things about the people who made them, and the way in which they lived.

General Pitt Rivers, born in 1827, was a soldier. He collected guns. Gradually he included other types of weapons, then tools, and then a wide range of everyday objects from other countries which he visited as a soldier. You can still see his collection in the Pitt Rivers Museum in Oxford.

When he was older, General Pitt Rivers inherited a large amount of land in the West Country which had many ancient archaeological sites on it. Each site was very carefully dug and everything that was excavated, however ordinary, was carefully recorded and its position was marked on a plan of the site. Unlike archaeologists before him, he insisted that everyday objects were as valuable as a guide to the past as precious ones were.

He opened a museum on his land which included an art gallery, a bandstand, a golf course, a racecourse, an open air theatre, a picnic area and a zoo. Today many museums offer a great deal more than just objects, but 100 years ago this was a great novelty.

Early collectors

We do not know who made the first collection of objects. But we do know that, as long ago as 280 BC, King Ptolemy of Egypt opened a museum in his palace in Alexandria.

In Britain, the Earl of Arundel was one of the first collectors. He bought back statues and other works of art from his travels to Italy in 1614 and put them on display in a special gallery in his house.

About the same time, John Tradescant started to collect objects of scientific interest, including plants and animal bones. When he died, his collection formed the beginning of the Ashmolean Museum, in Oxford, which is the oldest surviving museum in Britain.

John Tradescant, 1638, painted by Emanuel de Critz.

Wealthy collectors often met to discuss their collections. Special clubs and societies were formed. The Society of Antiquaries and the Society of Dilettanti were clubs formed over 200 years ago and they still exist today. ('Antiquaries' are people who collect things of the past. 'Dilettanti' is an Italian word for someone who loves beautiful things.)

Many of these early collections formed the beginnings of modern museums, art galleries and libraries. The British Museum, the largest and most visited museum in Britain, was started by Sir Hans Sloane, a scientist born in 1660. He collected rare books, fossils, precious stones, birds, plants, pictures, butterflies, shells and ancient remains from all over the world. When he died in 1753, Parliament granted some money so that the collection could be bought and displayed and everyone could see it.

Montague House, the home of the first British Museum

The Elgin Marbles: right or wrong?

The Parthenon was a great temple built in Athens, in Greece, about 400 years before Christ. It was dedicated to the goddess Athena and all the way round the top of the building were 111 magnificent marble carvings. Lord Elgin, who was the British Ambassador to Greece about 200 years ago, brought 56 of the carvings back to England from the Parthenon which was by then in ruins. Later, he sold them to the British Museum where they can still be seen.

Today, the Greek government would like the carvings back. But the British government is unwilling to return them.

The British government says that Lord Elgin was given permission by the Greeks to remove the carvings. They also say that if the marbles had not been taken away, they would now be ruined by the effects of weather and pollution which is particularly bad in Athens.

The Greeks say that Lord Elgin bribed officials to let him remove the carvings. They also say that tearing the carvings from the Parthenon made other parts of the building collapse.

Is a British museum the right place for something so important to the Greeks? Or is it a good idea that we are able to look at things which might otherwise only be seen if we are able to travel abroad? What do you think?

Going out to collect

One of the most exciting things about collecting is going out to hunt for new specimens.

Finding fossils, rocks and minerals

In the past, collectors of rocks, fossils and minerals have broken up rocks with a hammer and taken as many specimens as possible. Over the years, some areas in Britain have become seriously damaged by over enthusiastic collectors. For example, Lyme Regis in Dorset was once a very good area for collecting fossils. Now very few good fossils remain.

Today people realise that we must be more careful in looking after our environment. We should leave natural places for other people to enjoy. So if you collect fossils, rocks or minerals:

✗	Never use hammers to collect specimens.
✓	Only collect those which can be found loose on the ground.
✓	Collect only one specimen of each type so that there are some left for other people.

Knowing what to look for

It is important to know what you are looking for; look at pictures and museum displays of rocks and fossils which can be found in your area. When you go collecting, don't expect to see a whole fossil. Look for an edge or part of a fossil peeping out. If you are hunting for rocks, pick up pieces and weigh them in your hand. If one seems light for its size, there may be a space inside in which crystals have grown.

16

Useful equipment

Rocks, fossils and minerals are all collected in a similar way with equipment that can be used for all three. These are the things you will need:

Fine black waterproof felt-tip for marking the specimen.

Notebook for jotting down details on the spot. Give your specimen a number, and note the type of specimen and when and where you found it. It is a good idea to photograph the place to remind you where you found the specimen. This is especially important if you find something that turns out to be of scientific interest.

Rucksack to put everything in and leave your hands free.

Plastic bags for your specimens.

Plastic ice-cream containers for delicate finds. Use kitchen tissue paper for packing (cotton wool gets stuck on specimens and tissues fall apart too easily).

If at first you don't succeed . . .

The prehistoric remains of large mammals such as woolly rhino, bison and mammoth have been found in the ancient peat beds of Selsey Bill in Sussex. A few years ago, a local collector found half an elephant's thigh bone. The collector could see that it had been broken recently because the break was not discoloured. This meant that the other half might be nearby. Seven years later, the same collector struck lucky and found the other half!

Collecting pebbles

You don't need any special equipment to collect pebbles. Some pebbles, such as coloured quartz, are semi-precious stones, but they do not become semi-precious until they have been cut and polished by experts. Even then they are not likely to make you rich, so collect them for their colour and shape only.

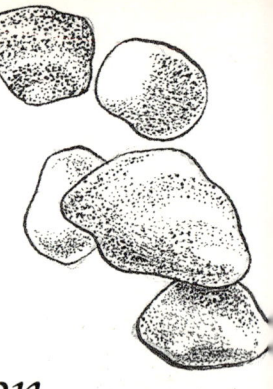

An environmental collection

If you live in the country or near a large park, you may like to collect seeds, leaves or grasses. But remember they should only be common types. If you live near the coast you could collect shells and seaweeds. In autumn, you could collect fallen leaves. Keep a notebook to record where you found them and try to find out which trees the leaves have come from. You could make notes about the trees to help you identify them more easily in the future. Use plastic ice-cream containers to put your leaves in. Later on, you could press them and keep them in a book.

Do's and don'ts for collecting outside

- ✓ Do tell a grown-up in your family where you are going.
- ✓ Do check the times of the tides if you are collecting on the shore.
- ✓ Do get permission to dig on private land.
- ✓ Do contact local clubs and societies so that you can go with adults who are interested in collecting. Your local museum and library will have the details.
- ✗ Never explore dangerous buildings, rubbish dumps, quarries or overhanging cliffs.
- ✗ Don't forget to clean up. Fill in any holes you may have dug and leave places as you found them so that other people can enjoy them.

Collecting bottles

The best places to find bottles are Victorian rubbish tips. But Victorian tips are often on private land and can be dangerous. If you particularly want to dig for bottles, go along to your local museum who will be able to put you in touch with a bottle collector's club. Many collectors buy and sell bottles at craft fairs and car boot sales which may be an easier way to build up your collection.

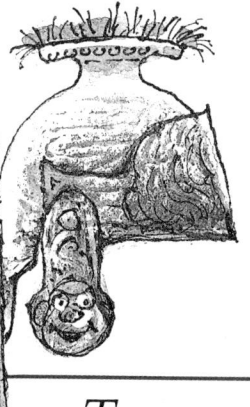

Treasure Trove

Most objects belong to the owner of the land on which they are found. But if the objects are made of gold or silver, special rules apply. Treasure that was lost or abandoned by the first owner is the property of the landowner, or sometimes, the finder. But if the first owner hid the objects with the idea of going back to find them, they are said to be Treasure Trove. Treasure Trove belongs to the Crown which means the country. It is offered to the British Museum in England, or the National Museums of Scotland.

If you find treasure, you should first tell the local police. An enquiry will then be held to decide if what you have found is Treasure Trove or not. As the finder, you would be offered the price the objects would fetch in a saleroom. If you kept your find a secret, you would be breaking the law.

Metal detectors: right or wrong?

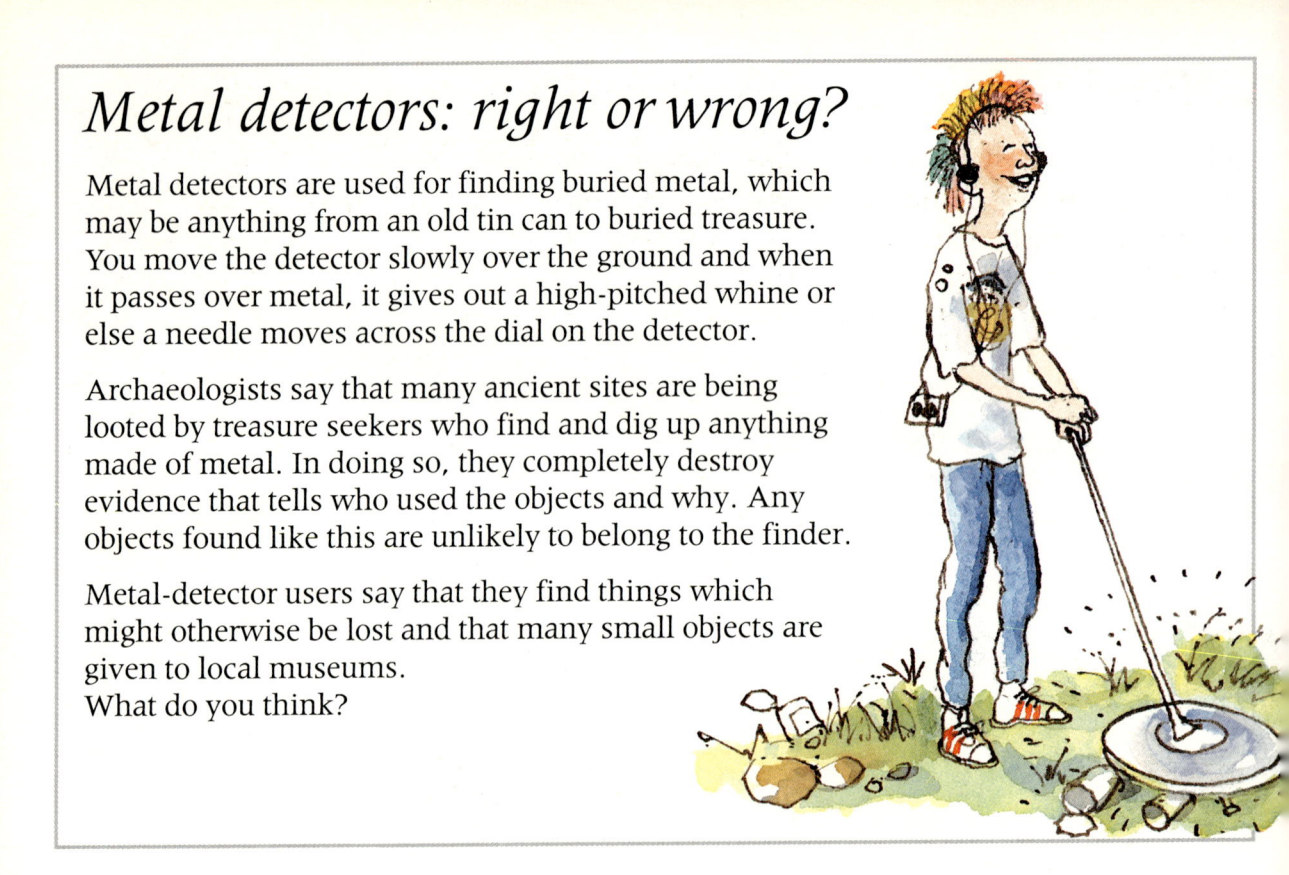

Metal detectors are used for finding buried metal, which may be anything from an old tin can to buried treasure. You move the detector slowly over the ground and when it passes over metal, it gives out a high-pitched whine or else a needle moves across the dial on the detector.

Archaeologists say that many ancient sites are being looted by treasure seekers who find and dig up anything made of metal. In doing so, they completely destroy evidence that tells who used the objects and why. Any objects found like this are unlikely to belong to the finder.

Metal-detector users say that they find things which might otherwise be lost and that many small objects are given to local museums.
What do you think?

Collecting rubbings

Some people 'collect' things such as church brasses, old gravestones and coal hole covers by taking rubbings of them. Sometimes the rubbings themselves become valuable, especially when the original object is lost for some reason. If you want to do some brass rubbing in a church, you'll need to ask permission first. Sometimes there is a small fee to pay.

Useful equipment

Pencil for noting details on the back of your rubbing of when and where you made it.

Rolls of paper brass rubbing paper is best, but thin, smooth layout paper available from art shops will do.

Scissors for cutting paper.

Cardboard tube for storing and carrying rubbings.

Masking tape (not Sellotape or Scotch Tape).

Brass rubbing sticks (available from art shops) are best, but thick black wax crayons will do.

Soft brush for cleaning surfaces.

Collecting with a tape-recorder

Tape-recordings of people's memories often form an extremely interesting part of museum collections. Not only do they give us details of everyday life which might otherwise be forgotten, but they also record the sound of people's voices and the accents in which they speak. Recordings of other kinds of sound are important, too. Just imagine how interesting the sound of a dodo (a kind of bird), which became extinct about 300 years ago, would be to scientists today.

If you want to record somebody's memories on a tape-recorder, it is very important to work out beforehand exactly what you want to ask. Write down possible questions in a notebook, for example:
'What did you feel like when you were told that you were going to live in another country?'
'How old were you at the time?'
'What can you remember about living in your old country?'

Don't forget to record the name of the person you are speaking to. Remember, not everyone likes talking about their memories, so ask permission beforehand. It is a good idea to practise on your family first!

What to do

1. Brush the surface clean if necessary.

2. Lay paper on the area or object you are going to rub and neatly fasten down the corners with masking tape.

3. Rub the area gently with a brass rubbing stick or wax crayon, to find out where edges are.

4. Rub all over, increasing the pressure to get a good black rubbing.

Remember, if the object you want to rub is on private land, get permission.

21

Getting sorted

Identifying your collection

Whatever you collect, you will need to identify items in your collection so that you can find out more about them. Your local bookshop, library or school library will have many well-illustrated books which will help you to do this. If you cannot find the information you need, write to or visit your local museum or gallery. (You can find out the best way to do this on page **46**.)

Classifying your collection

When you have identified your collection, you will need to sort different items into groups. This is called 'classifying': you group things together which have features in common. For example, if you collect shells you could sort them according to whether there is one part to the shell, or two. If you collect bottles you may like to group them according to the type of thing they once contained. For example, all bottles which contained drinks would be together. If you collect stamps, you will probably group them according to country, but there is no reason why you should not group them according to the pictures on them or even by colour.

Recording the information

Keep a notebook especially for your collection. Transfer into it any rough notes you may have made. List objects carefully, give them a number and record any further information you may find out. Try to list some of the same kind of information each time, so that you can make comparisons; for instance, where and when you found an item.

This is how an object would be recorded in a museum.

How and where the object was made.

Who used to own the object.

How the object came into the collection; was it found, given or bought?

Information about any repairs.

Any books used to identify the object, or documents (eg letters) associated with it.

Anything else which isn't mentioned elsewhere.

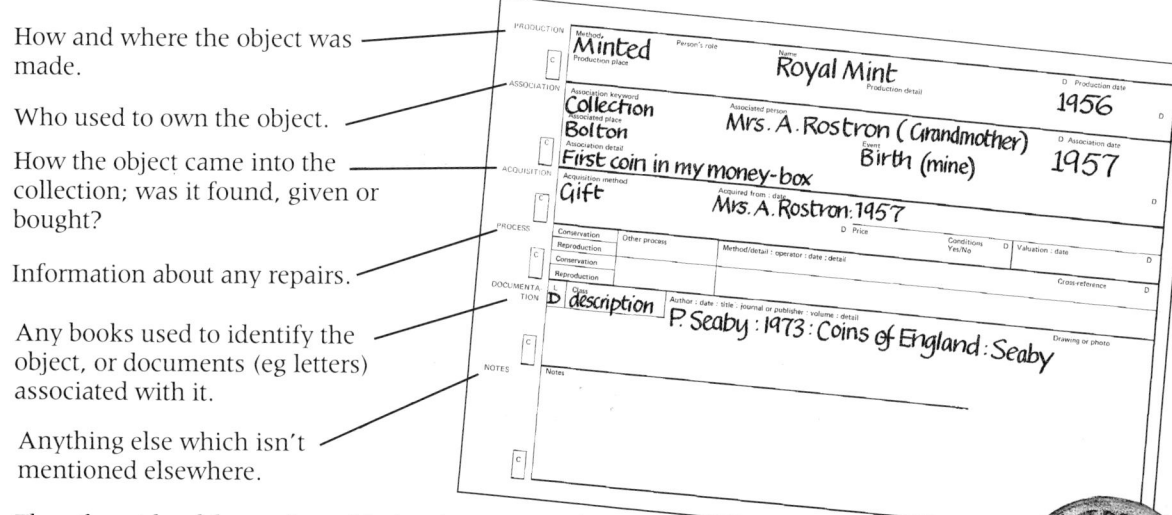

The other side of the card would give the name and a description of the object and the name of the person who identified it. A slightly different type of card would be used for something, like a fossil, which had been dug up.

Computers

In many museums the information on the card is transferred on to a computer. A computer enables people to deal with large amounts of information. You can ask a computer all sorts of questions without having to sift through all the details yourself. For example, a museum could use its computer to find out how many bottles in its collection are green, or how many were used to store drinks, or how many were found in a particular place, and where the bottles can be found in the museum store.

If you have a computer with a printer, you may like to create your own 'database' to store information about your collection. Ask your teacher to help. Before you start, try to think of the kind of questions you will want to ask. A computer can only sift through the information you have given it.

Caring for your collection

Once your collection is under way, you'll need to know how to store it in the right conditions and how to repair any damage.

Looking after paper

Football programmes, beer labels, wrappers and magazines are all printed on poor quality paper. This means they will turn yellow, go brittle and tear easily, and the colours will fade quickly.

- ✓ Do mount them with photographic corners and stick them in a scrap album.
- ✓ Do store your collection in dry conditions.
- ✗ Don't display your collection on the wall – sunlight will make the print fade.

Photographs

If you are lucky enough to have a collection of old photographs, you must take especially good care of them.

Do store photographs in flip albums made of polypropylene (ask in the shop).

Do store glossy prints separately – the surface is coated with gelatine which means they stick together very easily.

Do store negatives just as carefully as the prints. Use polypropylene wallets. Ask a photographic shop to help you choose a suitable type.

Don't put rubber bands around photographs – rubber bands are coated with sulphur which damages photographs.

Repairing damage

Did you find your most treasured wrapper or beer label screwed up in a rubbish bin? Don't despair – you can flatten it like this. (Practise on an old newspaper first.)

1. Spray the surface with water, using the type of spray bottle normally used for houseplants. Turn the nozzle to a fine spray. Watch out for drips!

2. Place the damp paper carefully in a polythene bag and seal. Remove from the bag after two to three days. The paper will now be very pliable.

3. Place carefully on a sheet of blotting paper and gently smooth out the creases.

4. Place another sheet of blotting paper on top and weigh down with something flat and heavy such as a pile of old magazines.

A disaster story with a happy ending

One winter's day, a heavy fall of snow lay on the leaking roof of Wootten Wawen church in Warwickshire. As it melted, it dripped straight on to a case below, containing a very old Bible. The case filled up to the brim like an aquarium. No one noticed for several days until a cleaner, dusting the surface of the case, saw ripples inside!

The Bible was removed. It was immediately sent to the Atomic Energy Laboratory at Harwell near Oxford because new technology can sometimes be very helpful with problems of restoration. There, the Bible was frozen to prevent any mould forming. Then it was dried under vacuum (which is a bit like the freeze-drying process used to make instant coffee). Finally the cover of the Bible, which was by then a bit mishapen, was repaired and the Bible was rebound. It is now as good as it was before.

A word about glue

If you need to use glue on paper either for repairs or mounting, be careful! Most modern glues are irreversible, which means that if you want to change the way you have mounted anything, or if you make a mess of any repair work, you won't be able to alter it.

×	Don't use glues such as Superglue, Bostik, PrittStick or Copydex.
×	Don't use sticky tape such as Sellotape or Scotch tape.
√	Do use glue which you can make yourself; it's the cheapest and the best.

Recipe for glue

50 g arrowroot, wheat flakes or rice flour (all available from a good supermarket) or ordinary flour
400 ml water

1. Mix together the ingredients.

2. Heat in a bowl set over a saucepan of hot water, stirring all the time until thick. Simmer for about 10 minutes.

Don't forget to tell an adult when you use a cooker

3. Leave to cool and store in a jar with a tight-fitting lid.

Storing stamps

Up to about 10 years ago, stamps were coated with glue made from natural materials like fish bones. They could be removed from envelopes by steaming. Today stamps are coated with modern plastic glues and are much more difficult to remove.

Collect stamps with the envelope they are attached to and store them in a plastic wallet. Or leave the stamp on the envelope, cut round it leaving a small margin and fix it in an album with a hinge. Try to buy 'Butterfly' hinges which are made up with animal glue.

Butterfly hinges

The Leonardo Cartoon

The Virgin and Child with St Anne and St John the Baptist, by Leonardo da Vinci is one of the most famous pictures in the world. You can see it in the National Gallery in London. It is called a cartoon which means it was a trial drawing for sorting out ideas before starting a painting. In 1987 the cartoon was very badly damaged by a man who fired at it with a gun. Although the picture was protected by bullet-proof glass, the force of the bullet caused a large dent in the picture. It took fifteen months to repair.

First, all the tiny splinters of glass were removed. Then the paper was shrunk back so that the drawing was flat again, and all the torn bits of paper were put back in their original positions. Finally the cartoon was carefully retouched with chalk and charcoal. Why not visit the Leonard Cartoon and see if you can spot where the bullet hit the picture?

Caring for pottery and glass

Have you ever wondered why there is so much pottery from ancient times in museums? The answer is, pottery does not rot away like leather and wood. But it breaks very easily which is why so much of the pottery in museums has been restored. Do you have a piece of pottery that you would like to mend? Here's how to do it.

Do ask a grown-up before using sharp blades

What's the damage?

Different methods and materials are used to mend different kinds of pottery. So first look at the damage. What is wrong? Has it been mended before? What type of pottery is it – soft earthenware or hard porcelain? Earthenware is soft and breaks easily: flowerpots are earthenware, for example. Porcelain is much harder and more brittle: delicate dinner plates and cups are often made of porcelain.

Now clean it up

All dirt and glues from earlier repairs must be removed so:

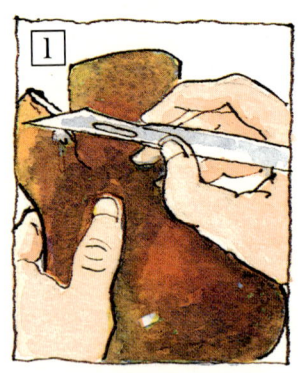

1. Use a sharp blade such as a sharp penknife or scalpel to scrape away glue from edges.

2. Wash in soapy water to remove dirt.

3. Remove rust staining with a rust remover such as Jenolite (you can buy it from hardware stores). Put it on with cotton buds.

4. Leave for 1–2 hours and rinse off with water. Repeat again if necessary.

The Portland Vase

The Portland Vase is one of the finest pieces of Ancient Roman glass in the world. Over 100 years ago, a drunken visitor to the British Museum smashed it into about 200 pieces. It was mended but recently it was discovered that the glue had turned yellow and had become brittle, so the vase was repaired again. It took nine months.

The vase was 'bandaged' with layers of damp blotting paper and a thin layer of plaster on top. This was to prevent it collapsing when the old glue was removed. Then the vase was placed in a special container called a 'desiccator' which softened the old glue.

The bandages were gradually peeled off and the separate pieces were pulled gently away and placed on a plan of the vase. The old glue was carefully scraped away from all the edges and the pieces were washed.

The vase was put back together again using two types of glue. All the missing spaces were filled with resin matched to the colour of the vase.

Why not go to see the Portland Vase in the British Museum? As you look at it, imagine how you would feel if you had one of the most famous objects in the world in pieces and it was up to you to put it together again.

Mending pottery and glass

Make sure the pottery or glass is free of dust and fluff.

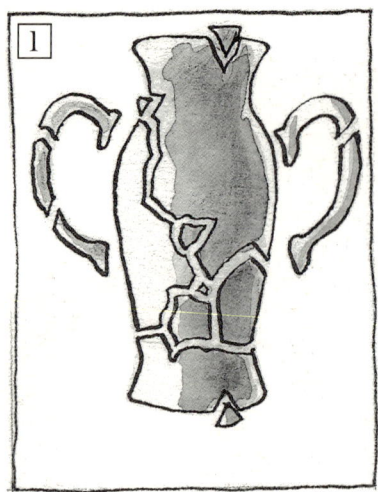  

1. Work out how you are going to stick the pieces together. (It is easiest to work from the base upwards and to stick small areas together to make larger sections.)

Do tell a grown-up when using glues. Many of them are *very poisonous*

2. Use fast-setting epoxy resins such as Araldite for porcelain and glass and Purcefix for earthenwarre. Use the glue according to the instructions on the tube or packet. Use as little as possible because too much will make it difficult to get a good join. Wipe away unwanted glue using kitchen paper.

3. If you are mending glass or porcelain, hold the pieces together with Sellotape or Magic Tape while the glue is setting. Use masking tape for earthenware because Sellotape might damage the delicate surface.

Retouching

Are there any missing areas? Fill in the small areas with Polyfilla. Match the colours carefully and paint with Cryla paints available from art shops.

In the past, broken objects which had parts missing were re-assembled, and the missing parts filled in, to make them look as complete as possible. Nowadays, objects are re-assembled so that at first glance they appear complete, but on closer inspection, you can tell the difference between the old parts and the new parts.

Caring for fossils, bones, shells and rocks

Wash fossils to remove any dirt. Dry them carefully with kitchen paper and pick off small parts of rock and other material with a large needle. Bones and shells should be soaked for a short time, and then gently scrubbed with an old soft toothbrush. Leave them to dry on kitchen paper. Use UHU, Lepage's polystyrene cement or balsa cement to stick broken bits back in place.

Fossils, bones and shells will get scratched and spoiled if you pile them into a drawer, so keep each one in a separate box, preferably with a lid, and label it on the outside. You can buy special cabinets of shallow drawers but they are quite expensive. Instead, you could divide an ordinary drawer into different sections for your collection.

Do tell a grown-up if you are going to use a sharp knife

Make your own display box
You will need:
Corrugated cardboard to make the partitions (an old cardboard box will do)

1. Measure the depth, width and length of the inside of your drawer.

2. Using a craft knife, cut two pieces of cardboard the same depth and width as your drawer.
Cut one piece of cardboard the same depth and length as your drawer.

3. Divide the longest piece into three and mark each third. At each mark, cut a slit into half the width.

Halfway along each short piece cut a slit into half the width.

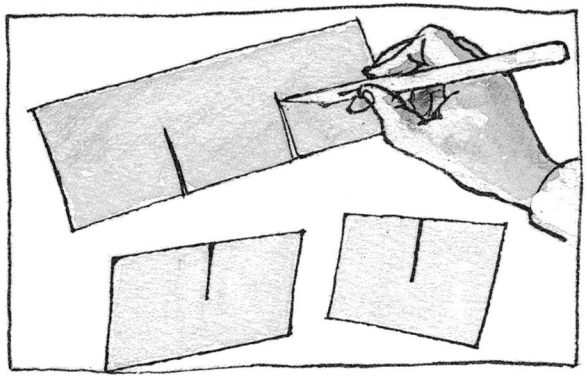

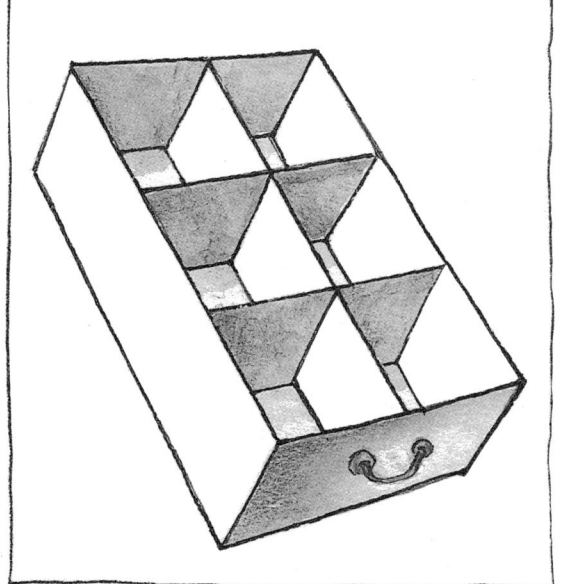

4. Slot the two short pieces into the long piece. If your cardboard is very thick, you will need to widen the slits. Fit the partitions into your drawer.

You could adapt this idea to make different-sized partitions to suit your collection.

Not everything has to be kept in boxes. Have you noticed how wet pebbles look much more beautiful than dry ones? Why not display your pebbles in water? Choose an interesting glass container. Put your pebbles into it and fill it up with water.

31

Keeping coins

Keep your coins looking their best by storing them properly. Too much handling may damage or tarnish the surface. Always handle coins by the edges, especially those in mint condition, or the salts in your skin will damage the surface.

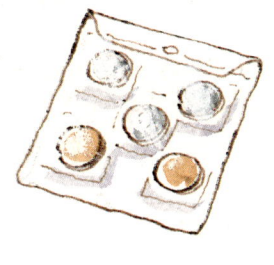

You can buy special coin cabinets which have drawers to hold coins of different sizes, but they tend to be rather expensive. You can also buy coin albums which hold coins in little pockets in transparent pages. They do not cost much to buy. Cheapest of all are coin envelopes which are bought in packets together with a strong cardboard box to put the envelopes in.

Other objects, like such as badges, might best be displayed on fabric. You could make a display board like this one:

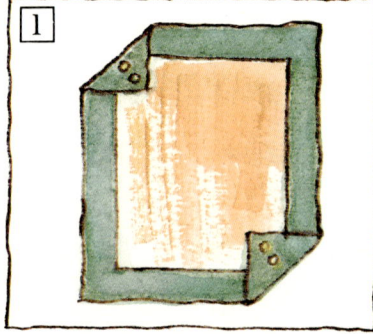

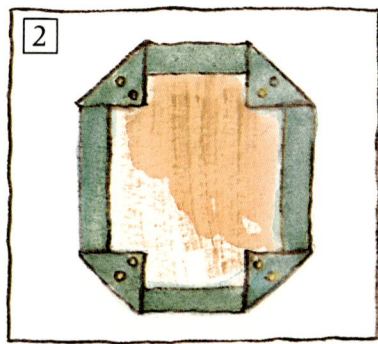

You will need:

A rectangular piece of chipboard or soft wood

A piece of fabric (felt or velvet would be ideal) which is big enough to allow for a generous wrap round on all sides

Some drawing pins with brass heads, and *a small hammer*

1. Take opposite corners of the fabric and pull tightly over the back of the board. Secure with drawing pins.

2. Repeat the process with the other corners, remember to pull the fabric tightly.

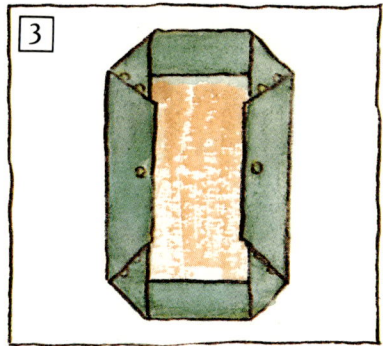

3. Take opposite sides of the fabric and pull tightly over the back of the board. Secure with a drawing pin halfway down each side.

4. Repeat the process with the other sides, still pulling tightly, then add more drawing pins all round.

Labelling your display

It's very important to label your display properly, even if it's only for your own enjoyment.

Think carefully about what you want to say about the exhibit you are labelling. Do you want to describe what it is made of? Where and when you found it? Who gave it to you? Is there anything special about it?

You could type or print neatly on to sticky labels. Draw a border round and centre the information like this for a really professional finish.

Perhaps you want your labels to stand up, like this one made from a folded piece of card.

Giving your collection a name

Have you thought of giving your collection a name? Some collections are named after their owners like The Pitt Rivers Museum in Oxford. Others tell us what type of collection they are, for example, the Exploratory Hands-on Science Centre in Bristol. Some have new words altogether like the Xperiment! Gallery in Manchester.

'Museum' comes from the Greek word 'mouseion'. In Ancient Greece, a museum was a temple to the goddesses of the arts who were called Muses. Each goddess had supporters (like football supporters) who often gave her gifts.

Curious cabinets

Some of the earliest collections were displayed in special cabinets called 'cabinets of curiosities'. Cabinets contained all sorts of wonderful, strange and curious objects. People competed with each other for the most interesting cabinet.

Sir Richard Worsley, who lived in Appuldurcombe House on the Isle of Wight about 200 years ago, had a cabinet specially made for all his small treasures. Sir Richard very carefully catalogued the contents. Here is what just one of the drawers contained: an antique sword and scabbard, a fibula (a brooch), a nail, a pair of compasses, a caltrop (a small spiked gadget, several were scattered on the ground to hold up the enemy), a large lance, a key, four priapuses (part of a male god), an image of Isis (an Egyptian god), a hatchet, a finger from a statue, a lion's head, a bronze, a bit (from a horse's harness), an incensory (for burning incense), a curious key, a key, a buckle, a Roman instrument, an instrument used in surgery, a small spear, a padlock, a ring with an inscription, a large fibula and the foot of a small statue.

This Chinese cabinet belonged to Charles Wade's grandmother (see page 9).

Make your own 'cabinet of curiosities'

You will need

At least 12 matchboxes of the same size

Gold paper fasteners

Glue, paint and coloured paper to decorate your cabinet

1. Make a hole in the front of each box and push a paper fastener through. The paper fasteners will be the handles for the 'drawers' in your cabinet.

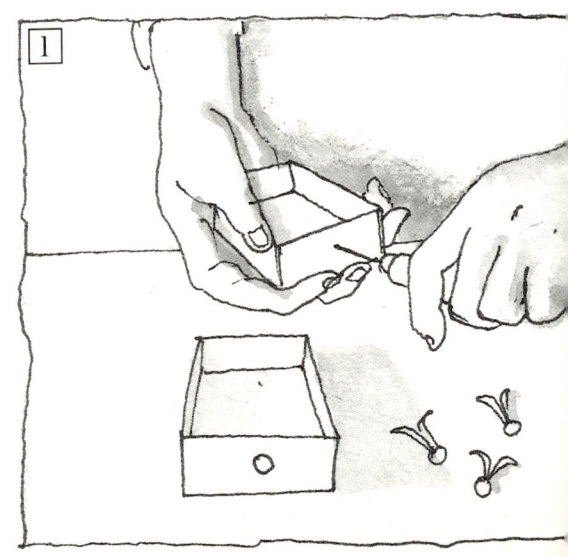

34

2. Put the boxes on top of each other. Try out different arrangements.

like this

or this

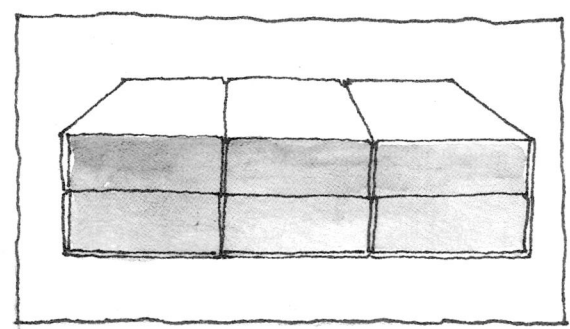

3. When you find an arrangement you like, stick the boxes together. Make sure the glue is only on the outside of the boxes, otherwise the 'drawers' won't open.

4. You can decorate the top, bottom and sides of your cabinet by sticking on patterned paper.

5. Decorate the front of each 'drawer' by painting, sticking on beads, sequins, scraps of paper or fabric.

Modern museums

Today, many museums have displays which depend on new technology. In the British Museum, for example, you can see a hologram of Lindlow Man who was murdered nearly 2000 years ago. A hologram is a 3D picture projected by a laser beam.

Many museums have 'hands on' displays where you can discover how things work by working models and equipment. There are displays like this in the Launch Pad at the Science Museum, London, the Science Factory at the Museum of Science and Engineering at Newcastle, and the Xperiment! Gallery at the Greater Manchester Museum of Science and Industry.

There are also museums which show us how people used to live, such as the York Castle Museum, and Abbot Hall Museum in Kendal, Cumbria, where whole rooms or shops are reconstructed, using furniture and objects from the past.

A reconstructed candle factory in Blists Hill Museum, Ironbridge, Shropshire.

There are working museums where the collections are in everyday use in their natural surroundings such as the Ironbridge Gorge Museum, near Telford, in Shropshire, or the Black Country Museum which has a colliery, with mine shafts and a miners' village.

The Director is in charge of the whole museum.

Keepers are in charge of different departments. They find out more about the objects in their care and write about them too.

Conservators look after the objects and repair them if necessary.

Designers help to decide how the collections should be displayed.

Office staff type all the letters and answer the telephones.

Behind the scenes

If you want to get the most out of museums, it helps to know how they are run.

The displays on show in museums are just a small part of the collection. Only the most interesting or valuable things are displayed. The rest are kept in the museum stores where they are available for people to study.

Several hundred people may work in a large museum. Here is what some of them do.

Warders look after the visitors in the galleries and are responsible for security.

...ation Officers are teachers ...work in a museum instead ...school.

...ners make sure that the ...seum is clean and tidy for ...ning time.

A one-man show

There are hundreds of small museums where just one or two people do everything!

The Swaledale Folk Museum in Reeth, North Yorkshire, is a museum about the traditional life of the people who live in that area. It was started by Mr Donald Law who still runs it. He does everything from making the show cases and models for the displays to the cleaning. He even built the extension to the museum!

37

The laboratory

Many large museums and galleries have laboratories with powerful modern equipment, some of which wouldn't be out of place in an atomic research station or a well-equipped hospital.

The research scientists who work in the laboratory try to find out more about the objects in their care. They try to find answers to questions like: What is it made of? Where did the materials come from? How was it made? When was it made? Is it a forgery? They can usually discover a great deal about an object by examining it under a powerful microscope, but sometimes special methods are used to find out more.

How old is it?

Scientists use different ways of finding out how old something is. Radiocarbon dating can be used to tell the age of objects that were once alive, such as bones or seeds. Everything which was once alive contains tiny amounts of radiocarbon. By measuring the amount remaining in an object, scientists can tell how long it has been since the object was alive.

Dendrochronology (the study of tree rings) can be used to find out the age of wood. It is usually used to date large pieces of wood such as parts of an old wooden building or a boat.

Objects, such as clay pots, which were heated when they were made throw out a special light called thermoluminescence (say 'thermo-lume-in-essence'). The amount of thermoluminescence can be measured. The stronger the light, the older the pot will be.

How was it made?

X-rays can show the inside of an object and reveal how it was made. Ultra violet light can sometimes tell scientists when something has been made to look older than it is, so it is useful for detecting whether something is a fake.

When looked at in ordinary light, the vase appears unbroken.

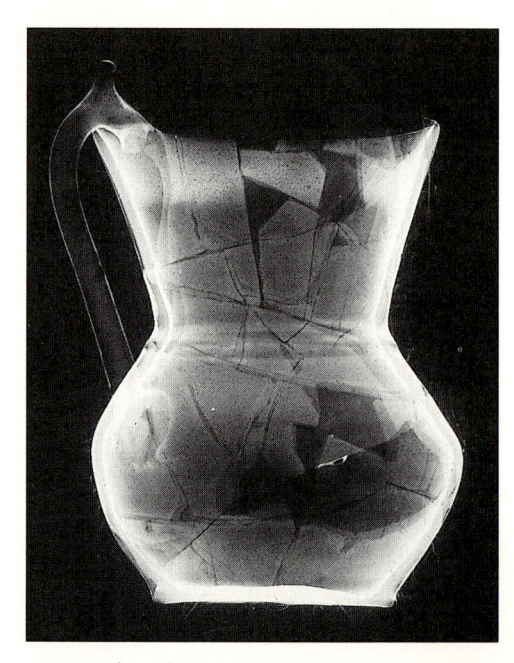

An X-ray shows that it is made up of broken fragments.

Fabulous fakes

Fakes and forgeries are made to cheat people. Everthing, from ancient remains and rare stamps to paintings and jewels, has been faked. Fakes are detected by being shown to be of the wrong date, or being made in the wrong way or made of unsuitable materials. It isn't easy to fool experts, but sometimes mistakes are made. Works of art have even been declared fakes when they are genuine!

The man who never was

Ever since scientists realised that human beings are descended from apes, the hunt has been on to find the missing link – an animal half way between human beings and apes.

In 1912, parts of an unusual skull and jawbone were found in a gravel pit at Piltdown in Sussex. The man who found them, Charles Dawson, a lawyer and amateur archaeologist, sent them to the Natural History Museum. When the pieces were fitted together, it looked as though the missing link had been found. Later some more bones were found. Scientists everywhere were very excited.

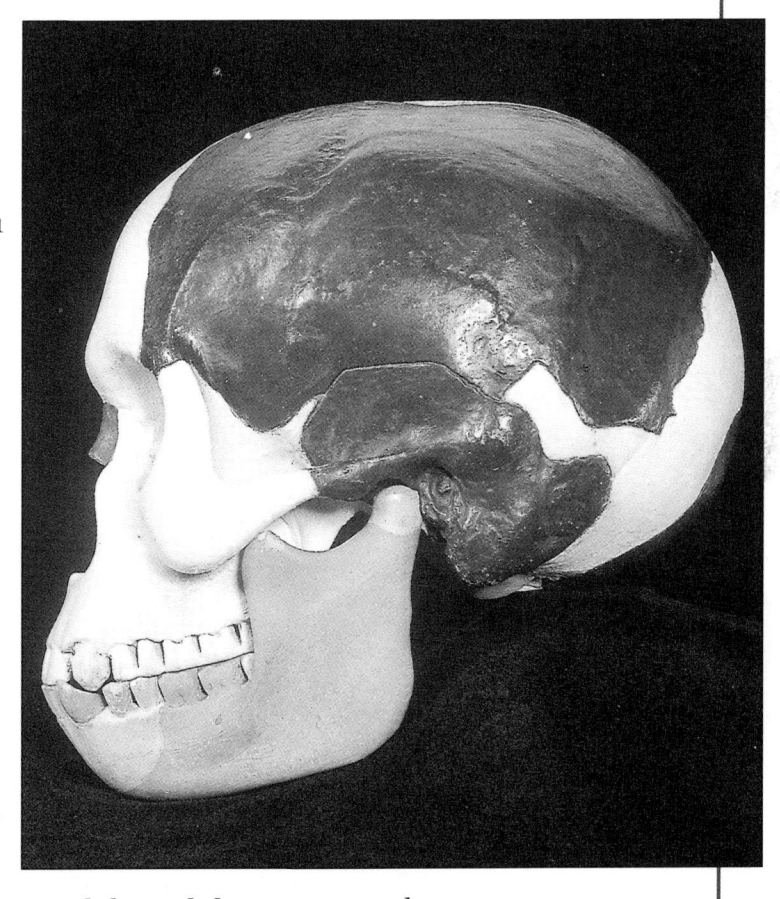

Nearly forty years later, it was discovered that Piltdown Man, as he came to be called, was a fake. The teeth had been deliberately filed down and the skull and jawbone had been stained to make it look ancient. In fact, after tests, it was discovered that the skull belonged to modern man and the jaw to a young orang-utan. To this day no one knows for certain who did it, but many people now believe it was Charles Dawson, with help from someone else, perhaps Sir Arthur Keith who was a famous anthropologist at the time. (An anthropologist is someone who studies human beings.)

Billies and Charlies

Billie and Charlie were two London workmen who lived in Victorian times. While they were working, they dug up a genuine antique which they sold for a large sum of money. No more discoveries came their way so they decided to make a few of their own.

They used a mixture of copper and lead to make medallions, daggers, vases and various other objects. Today, no one would be fooled – Billie and Charlie made the forgeries up as they went along! This picture of one of their medallions shows some of their mistakes. The date is in Arabic numerals instead of Roman numerals. The helmet is unlike anything in a museum, and the inscription is gibberish!

Today, Billies and Charlies are valuable in their own right and the Museum of London has a large collection of them.

The case of Hans van Meegeren

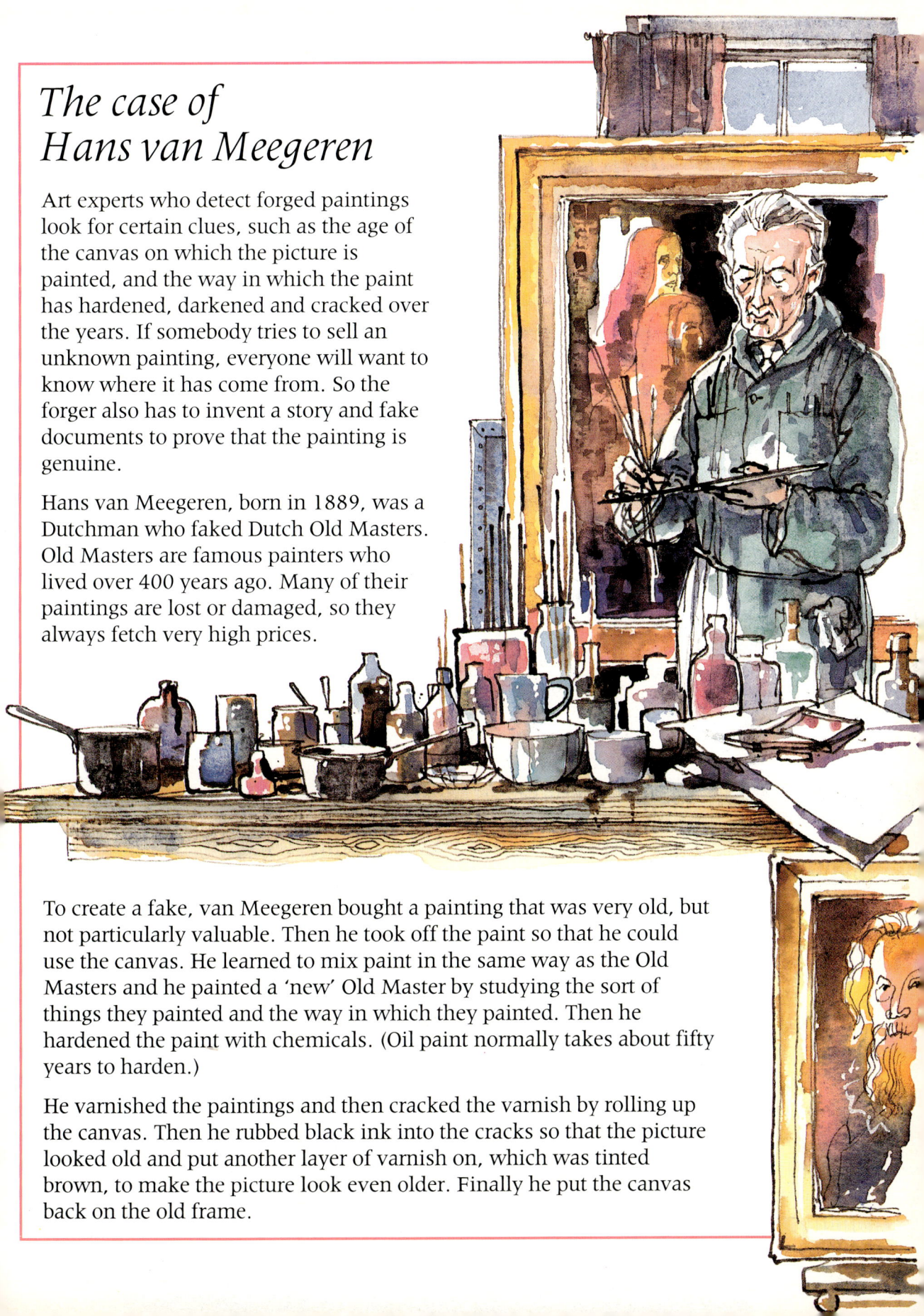

Art experts who detect forged paintings look for certain clues, such as the age of the canvas on which the picture is painted, and the way in which the paint has hardened, darkened and cracked over the years. If somebody tries to sell an unknown painting, everyone will want to know where it has come from. So the forger also has to invent a story and fake documents to prove that the painting is genuine.

Hans van Meegeren, born in 1889, was a Dutchman who faked Dutch Old Masters. Old Masters are famous painters who lived over 400 years ago. Many of their paintings are lost or damaged, so they always fetch very high prices.

To create a fake, van Meegeren bought a painting that was very old, but not particularly valuable. Then he took off the paint so that he could use the canvas. He learned to mix paint in the same way as the Old Masters and he painted a 'new' Old Master by studying the sort of things they painted and the way in which they painted. Then he hardened the paint with chemicals. (Oil paint normally takes about fifty years to harden.)

He varnished the paintings and then cracked the varnish by rolling up the canvas. Then he rubbed black ink into the cracks so that the picture looked old and put another layer of varnish on, which was tinted brown, to make the picture look even older. Finally he put the canvas back on the old frame.

Make a fake

Scagliola (say scally-o-la) is fake marble. It was very popular about 200 years ago when fashionable houses had columns, fireplaces and even whole rooms made of it. You can tell the difference between scagliola and real marble because marble is always very cold to touch, but scagliola feels warmer.

You will need

Rubber gloves

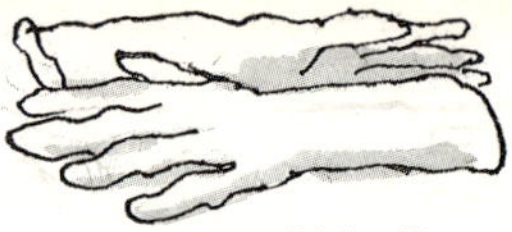

Old knife and sp

Cooking oil

One kilo of builder's plaster (not Polyfilla)

Water

Powder paint in two colours (contrasting colours work bes

Two bowls

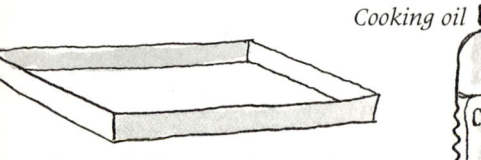

Large shallow container such as the lid of a large square biscuit tin or an old baking tray

1. Wipe the inside of the container with oil. Make sure it is well covered or your scagliola will be difficult to remove.

2. Wear rubber gloves when handling the plaster. Put about two thirds of the plaster into a bowl. Add some dry powder paint in one colour to the plaster. (The lighter the colour, the more you will need to use. The colour should look strong.) Mix thoroughly.

3. Add water, a little at a time. The mixture should end up looking like soggy dough. If it is too wet it will be difficult to handle and the colours may run together.

4. In another bowl mix the rest of the plaster and the second colour and add water to make a soggy dough as before.

5. Break off small pieces of the 'dough' and flatten them slightly. Place the different colours together. Now press the whole lot together into a big ball and flatten it out again. Cut into strips a centimetre or two wide. Shuffle the strips into a different order and then squash them together again. Repeat twice more.

6. Lay the marbled mixture in the container. Press down as evenly as possible. It should be about 2 cm thick.

Leave it overnight.

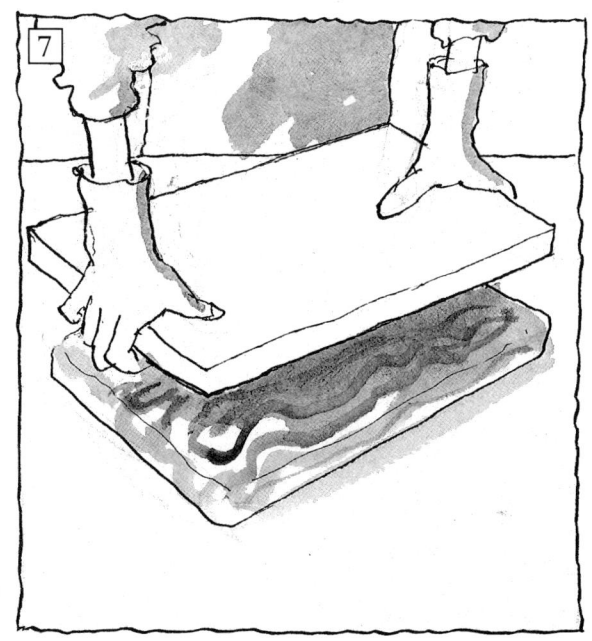

7. To remove the scagliola, twist the container slightly. If the scagliola won't come out, try tapping the container gently.

8. When you become an expert, experiment with more colours. Try dipping string in a sloppy mixture of paint and plaster and laying it in 'veins' on the bottom of the box. Remove the string and add the rest of the mix in the usual way.

How to find out more

Sooner or later you will want to find out more about your collection. The first place to look is the reference department of your local library. There you will find encyclopedias, atlases, maps, dictionaries and directories. Different encyclopedias list information in different ways. And dictionaries are not just about the meanings of words – there are dictionaries of people too. So try to find time to browse. If you have any difficulty finding out what you want, ask the librarian – they are there to help you.

The books in the reference section are for use in the library only. You may not take them home because they must always be there for everyone to use. Of course you can borrow any book you like from the lending library. Did you know that, even if your library does not have a particular book, the librarian may be able to order it from another library? Your teacher may also be able to borrow a book for you through the schools library service.

The reference library also stores information in other ways, for example, on microfilm and on computer.

An index – the secret weapon

An index is a very useful tool for finding out what you want. In a book, it is an alphabetical list of topics, people and places mentioned in the book and it tells you on which page you can find that information. Sometimes the information you need may be in more than one place. Try the index in this book and find out. Look up how you might mend pottery. Try looking under 'pottery' first. Then try under 'repairing'

Large encyclopedias contain so much information that they need to be published in several books, called volumes. Sometimes there is an index for each volume, but more often there is a separate book, containing the index to all the volumes.

Libraries have indexes, too. Supposing you want a book about coins but you do not know its name. Find the subject index: the librarian will tell you where it is kept. It may be on cards, in a book, or on a computer. Look up 'coins'. If the index is on cards, it will list a number for coins. You then look up that number in the library catalogue which will give you a list of all the books in the library on coins and where to find them.

An index on computer will list the books on coins and where to find them in the library. The computer might also be able to tell you if the book has been taken out by someone else, or if it is in another local library.

If you know who wrote a particular book but are not sure what it is called, or when you want to find more books by the same author, you can use the author catalogue, on cards, in a book, or on computer. Look up the name of the author. The catalogue will list all the books written by that person.

Libraries also store large scale maps of your area which can be useful, for example, for fossil hunting. They have various magazines about collecting which you can browse through, and information about local clubs and societies you might want to join.

45

Getting information from a museum

Do you need special advice about your collection that you cannot get from the library? Or do you need information from a museum or gallery for a school project? Write a letter!

First, make sure you send it to the right person. If the museum or gallery is a large one, send your letter to the education department. If they cannot answer your query, they will pass it on to the right person. If the museum is a small one, address your letter to the Curator.

This type of letter sends museum people mad!

> Dear Sir/Madam,
> Please send me all the information you have about houses through the ages. If you have any other information that would interest me, please send that too.

Make sure you know exactly what you want and ask for it clearly, like this.

> Dear...,
> I am doing a project on houses in Tudor times. Please send me any information you may have on how houses were built then, or a publications list with anything which might help me, marked on it. Does your museum have any information about Tudor houses which I could see during my visit? Thank you for your help.

If you get a helpful letter back, a letter of thanks is always welcome.

Many museums and galleries have special days when they will give advice or answer questions. Telephone them and find out.

Getting the most out of a visit

Does your mind go blank when you visit a very large museum or gallery for the first time? Don't worry! The secret is don't try to see everything in one go!

Decide what you want to see. It might be a special exhibition, or a collection of something which you already know a bit about, or perhaps something which is totally new to you.

Look for a plan of the museum or gallery. It will tell you what's on offer and where to find it. A small museum may not have a plan so ask at the information desk.

Join the club

Your local library or museum will have a list of local societies like bottle collecting clubs, geological societies and stamp collectors' clubs. Many of them have special sections for young people. If they don't, why not ask them to make one?

Many museums, galleries and libraries run clubs for young people or organise activities during the school holidays. Telephone and find out.

You may like to know about the following:

The Ephemera Society 12 Fitzroy Square, London W1P 5HQ
The British Matchbox Label and Booklet Society Contact the Membership Secretary, Department HH, 3 Langton Close, Norwich NR5 8RU
Geologists Association, Burlington House, Piccadilly, London W1V 0JU
Young Archaeologists Club. Contact Kate Pretty, New Hall, Cambridge CB3 0P7
Keep is the junior section of English Heritage who look after many ancient monuments in England. *Cadw* looks after buildings in Wales. Write to *English Heritage*, Keysign House, 429 Oxford St, London W1R 2HD
Young National Trust is the junior section of The National Trust who look after many historic houses in England and Wales. There is also *The National Trust for Scotland*, write to 36 Queen Anne's Gate London SW1H 9AS.

Read all about it

There are various magazines on sale which specialise in collecting such as:

Coin News, Coin Monthly, Gibbons Stamp Monthly, Stamp and Coin Mart, Stamps, Stamp Magazine, Model Collector, Collecting Scale Models, Clocks.

Museums and Galleries in Great Britain and Ireland, published by British Leisure Publications and brought up to date every year can be bought in large newsagents or borrowed from most libraries. It has a subject index which means you can find out which museums have collections that particularly interest you. It is especially useful if you are on holiday and want to know what's in the area.

Places mentioned in this book

Some of the museums and historic houses mentioned here are open all the year round, some only on certain days. It is best to telephone before you set out.

Appuldurcombe House Wroxall, near Ventnor, Isle of Wight
Ashmolean Museum Beaumont Street, Oxford
Black Country Museum Tipton Road, Dudley
The Bodleian Library Oxford OX1 3BG
The British Museum Great Russell Street, London, WC1B 3DG
The Brooking Collection Trust Woodhay House, White Lane, Guildford, Surrey, GU4 8PU
The Dog Collar Museum Leeds Castle, Maidstone, Kent, ME17 1PL
Erdigg Park Wrexham, Clwyd, LL13 0YT
The Exploratory Hands-On Science Centre Bristol Old Station, Temple Meads, Bristol
The Farmland Museum 50 High Street, Haddenham, near Ely Cambridgeshire, CB6 3XB
Greater Manchester Museum of Science and Industry Liverpool Road Station, Liverpool Road, Castlefield, Manchester M3 4JP
Blists Hill, part of the *Ironbridge Gorge Museum* The Wharfage, Ironbridge, Telford, Shropshire TF8 7AW
Museum in Docklands contact *Museum of London*, London Wall, London, EC2Y 5HN
Museum of Science and Engineering Blandford House, West Blandford Street, Newcastle-on-Tyne NE1 4JH
The National Gallery Trafalgar Square, London, WC2N 5DN
Natural History Museum Cromwell Road, South Kensington, SW7 5BD.
Pitt Rivers Museum South Parks Road, Oxford, OX1 3PP
The Robert Opie Collection Albert Warehouse, Gloucester Docks, Gloucester, GL1 2EH
The Science Museum Exhibition Road, South Kensington, London, SW7 2DD
Snowshill Manor near Broadway, Gloucestershire, WR12 7JU
Swaledale Folk Museum Reeth, North Yorkshire, D11 4RT
Ulster Folk and Transport Museum Cultra Manor, Holywood, County Down, Northern Ireland, BT18 0EU
York Castle Museum Eye of York, YO1 1RY

Index

Appuldurcombe House, Wroxall 34, 37
Arundel, Earl of 14

badges 32
Ballyveridagh School 10
Bodleian Library, Oxford 4
bottles 7, 19, 22
The British Matchbox Label and Booklet Society 47
Brooking, Charles 9
buttons 6

cabinet of curiosities 34–5
church brasses, rubbings of 20
classifying your collection 22
clubs for collectors 47
coins 3, 12, 32
computers 23, 44, 45
crime, museum of 8

Dawson, Charles 39
Delanoy, Craig 8
dendrochronology 38
displays, displaying 31, 32, 33, 37
dog collars 6
d'Orléans, Philippe 6

Elgin Marbles 15
Ellmers, Chris 11
encyclopedias 44, 45
environmental collection 18
The Ephemera Society 47

fakes and forgeries 39–43
family museums 12
fossils, bones, rocks and minerals, 3, 16–17, 31

Geologists Association 47
glue 26
gravestones, rubbings of 20

'hands on' displays 33, 36

identifying your collection 22
index 45

Johnson, Dr John 4, 5

Keith, Sir Arthur 39
labelling your display 33
laboratories, museum 38
Law, Donald 37
Leonardo Cartoon 27
Lindlow Man 36
London docks 11

magazines 47
mammals, prehistoric 17
matchbox labels 5
memories 7, 21
metal detectors 20
museums 8–14, 36–8, 46
  Abbot Hall Museum, Kendal 36
  Ashmolean Museum, Oxford 14
  Black Country Museum 36
  Bodleian Library, Oxford 4
  British Museum 14, 19, 29, 36, 47
  Brooking Collection 9, 47
  Dog Collar Museum, Leeds Castle 6, 47
  Erdigg Park, Wrexham 12, 47
  Exploratory Hands on Science Centre, Bristol 33, 47
  Farmland Museum 8, 47
  Greater Manchester Museum of Science and Industry 33, 36, 47
  Ironbridge Gorge Museum, Telford 36, 47
  Museum in Docklands 11, 47
  Museum of London 11, 40, 47
  Museum of Science and Engineering, Newcastle 36, 47
  National Gallery, London 27, 47
  National Museum of Scotland 19
  Natural History Museum, London 39
  Pitt Rivers Museum, Oxford 13, 33, 47
  Robert Opie Collection, Gloucester 4, 47
  Science Museum, London 36
  Snowshill Manor 9
  Swaledale Folk Museum 37
  Ulster Folk and Transport Museum 10

York Castle Museum 36

naming your collection 33

Old Masters, forging of 41
Opie, Robert 4

packaging and advertising material 4
paintings, forged 41
paintings, restoring 27
paper, looking after 24
Parthenon 15
pebbles 3, 18, 31
photograph collections, storing 24
Piltdown Man 39
Pitts Rivers, Lieutenant General 13
Portland Vase 29
pottery and glass, mending 28, 30
printed ephemera 4, 5
Ptolemy, King of Egypt 14

radiocarbon dating 38
recording information 23
reference library 44
repairing and restoring 25–30
retouching pottery and china 30
rubbings 7, 20–1

scagliola (fake marble) 42–3
Selsey Bill fossils 17
shells 3, 18, 31
Sloane, Sir Hans 14
Society of Antiquaries 14
Society of Dilettanti 14
stamps 3, 27

tape-recordings 21
thermoluminescence, measuring 38
Tradescant, John 14
Treasure Trove 19

Van Meegeren, Hans 41

Wade, Charles 9
Wootten Wawen church Bible 25–6
Worsley, Sir Richard 34

X-rays 38

Young Archaeologists Club 47
Young National Trust 47

First published 1991
A & C Black (Publishers) Limited
35 Bedford Row, London WC1R 4JH

ISBN 0–7136–3470–7

© 1991 A & C Black (Publishers) Limited

A CIP catalogue record for this book is available from the British Library.

Acknowledgements

For my mother who first took me to the Fitzwilliam Museum in Cambridge when I was very young.

The author would like to thank the staff of Chichester District Museum, Chichester County Library, West Dean College, the pupils of Townhill Middle School, Southampton and all the museums and advisors who have helped with this book.

Illustrations by Robert Geary, B. L. Kearley Ltd.

Photographs reproduced permission of: p4 Robert Opie Collection; p7, 19 Maggie Murray; p8 Farmland Museum; p9, 34 National Trust; p10 Ulster Folk and Transport Museum; p11 Museum of London Docklands Collection; p13 The Pitt Rivers Museum, University of Oxford; p14 (top) Ashmolean Museum; p14, 15, 29, 38 reproduced by courtesy of the British Museum; p27 reproduced by courtesy of the Trustees, The National Gallery London; p36 Blists Hill Museum; p39 Natural History Museum; p40 Museum of London.

Apart from any fair dealing for the purposes of research or private study, or criticism or review, as permitted under the Copyright, Designs and Patents Act, 1988, this publication may be reproduced, stored or transmitted, in any form or by any means, only with the prior permission in writing of the publishers, or in the case of reprographic reproduction in accordance with the terms of licences issued by the Copyright Licensing Agency. Inquiries concerning reproduction outside those terms should be sent to the publishers at the above named address.

Filmset by August Filmsetting, Haydock, St Helens
Printed and bound in Italy by Amadeus